WHERE'S MY F**KING UNICORN?

A GUIDE TO LIFE, YOUR UNICORN & EVERYTHING

WHERE'S MY

A GUIDE TO
LIFE, YOUR
UNICORN &
EVERYTHING

F**KING
UNICORN?

MICHELLE GORDON

AMMONITE
PRESS

**THIS BOOK IS DEDICATED TO ALL MY UNICORN SEEKING FRIENDS.
LET'S HAVE A PARTY WHEN WE FIND THEM!**

First published 2017 by
Ammonite Press
an imprint of Guild of Master Craftsman Publications Ltd
Castle Place, 166 High Street, Lewes, East Sussex, BN7 1XU,
United Kingdom
www.ammonitepress.com

Reprinted 2018

ISBN 978 1 78145 308 7

Publisher: Jason Hook
Designer: Robin Shields
Editor: Jamie Pumfrey
Illustrator: Kate Chesterton

Colour reproduction by GMC Reprographics

Printed and bound in Turkey

Contents

WHAT THE FUCK IS MY UNICORN?

You've read the books, attended the seminars, done the chanting and burned the incense, but you're still waiting for your fucking unicorn. You've been searching and searching, but that damned unicorn is still nowhere to be found.

WHY?

Well, that's what I hope to address in this book.

ANOTHER FUCKING SELF-HELP BOOK?

Nope. This is the book that tells you why, despite reading a million self-help books, attending seminars and watching webinars, your life still has not changed/taken off/become wildly successful. This is the book that will actually make self-help books **WORK** for you.

But why should you read it?

Because it might help you to use the knowledge you already have and change your life. Finally.

I might not be an expert, but I have lived it. I have experienced it. I have seen it. And I want to share it with you.

I will reference stuff that I think is actually useful, but my intention isn't to send you off on a wild self-help-treasure-goose-egg hunt, so only watch the videos or read the books I suggest if they really grab you and if you honestly think they will help. Or, you know, if you're really bored and need something just to pass the time. It'll make a change from watching cat videos.

You may be wondering what the hell I mean by finding your unicorn. And that's a fair point. The thing is, your unicorn is not likely to be the same as mine or the same as your best friend's. You may even have lots of unicorns, not just one. So ...

WHAT IS YOUR UNICORN?

My unicorn is living life as an author. A writer. My unicorn is being able to afford to write books as well as eat and keep a roof over my head. It's spending time with my favourite people. It's travelling the world and experiencing new sights, sounds and smells. It's having a good supply of fluffy socks and craft projects. As you can see, that's really quite a lot of different unicorns.

Your unicorn might be:

• playing your guitar on a stage in front of thousands of people;

• the time and space to meditate every day;

• having a passionate relationship;

• the feeling of security that you have enough money;

• the freedom to pursue your passions.

Your unicorn is likely to change over time, as you and your priorities change. Your unicorn at the age of seven could be very different from your unicorn at the age of 17 or 27. One of the biggest reasons why people don't change their lives is that they have no idea what their unicorn is. They haven't defined it. How can you find something if you don't know what it looks like, feels like, smells like or sounds like?

So, say it now, out loud, what your unicorn is. If you have many, list them. If you have just one, yell it from the rooftops. Then read on to discover how to find it.

WHERE'S MY FUCKING UNICORN?

Method In Your Madness

Even if we believe that we have no routine or structure in our lives, that we are creative souls who go wherever the ideas take us, we most certainly will have methods or rituals that work for us. Most self-help books go into detail about exercises and routines that we must adopt if we want to be successful – and suggest that if we are unsuccessful in adopting them, we will also be unsuccessful in our endeavours.

THAT'S JUST CRAP!

What they should be saying is that not all methods or rituals in any given book will work for you. Try them out, see what fits and get rid of what doesn't. Or modify them and make them your own. The most important thing is to find what works for **YOU**. And then run with it.

I have wanted to be a writer since I was eight years old. It was then that I started writing short stories, and at the age of 11, I started writing poetry. I dreamed of being an author. Of writing books. Full-length, proper books. But I was useless at researching subjects, and it seemed that good writers always did their research. I was impatient, and I had a short attention span, so the idea of taking the average three to ten years to write a book put me off, because I knew I wouldn't stay focused on one thing for that long.

I also hated plotting. If I knew how the story ended I would get bored and wouldn't bother writing it. I started an amazing story as a teenager, and it was going well until I had a bright idea for the ending. I wrote the ending then never wrote the middle, because there seemed little point in bothering – my interest in telling the story had gone. None of these things were conducive to living a successful life as a published author.

But then I discovered NaNoWriMo, the movement that encourages you to write a book in a month. All you have to do is write 1,667 words a day for 30 days.

Well, that took care of the attention-span issue – I was sure I could focus for a month. It also introduced the concept of being a 'pantser', the writer who flies by the seat of their pants, who does not plot, who just rolls with the characters and lets the words tumble out onto the page. Perfect!

Armed with my ancient laptop and its missing L key and a vague idea, I wrote solidly for two months and finished my very first full-length novel.

Suddenly, it was possible for me to be an author. Because I had found my method. To many writers, I know this must sound like madness, but it works for me: a crazy deadline, a vague idea and a laptop. It doesn't work for all writers, however. Some need to plot, need to research, need time and need the publishing deal with a big press. And so they must find their own ways to make that happen.

Whether you are a plotter or a pantser, there is no right or wrong route, and neither is better than the other. It doesn't matter what the method is, as long as it works for **YOU**. Finding your method is very much a trial-and-error kind of thing. Try a whole bunch of stuff, and don't be afraid to **FAIL**!

The failures help you to understand what doesn't work for you. Discard those methods and just keep the stuff that works. It's really that simple, but you need to be open to trying it. There's no point in reading a shitload of books, then going ...

'Nah, they won't work for **ME**. I'm **DIFFERENT**.'

Yeah, whatever. Try it. Play with it. You might be pleasantly surprised, and you might just think, *Yup, knew that was going to be a no-no*, but it doesn't matter either way; it's just a process of elimination to find the perfect method for you.

The Belief Con-ception

Our beliefs shape who we are, what we do, how we think, act, feel and how we present ourselves to the world. So they're pretty fucking important. You would think that they would be formed when we are aware enough to make conscious choices and decisions. But no, they form before the age of seven, before we actually have any idea of what the hell is going on, and then we basically much live with them for the rest of our lives.

But we don't **HAVE** to.

Beliefs are **NOT** set in stone. They **CAN** be changed. And if you are serious about changing your life, a good hard look at your beliefs is an important step in doing that.

What do you believe? What is your truth? What do you stick by day in day out? There are sooooo many books out there about reprogramming your mind, about your thoughts becoming things, about the power of attraction, about manifesting our dreams and so on. But we still don't have what we want. We're still broke. Our lives still suck.

We still don't have our fucking unicorn.

That's because no matter how many books we read, our beliefs haven't changed. Why? Because changing our beliefs takes work. Yes, actual effort. We have been living and breathing our beliefs all our lives, so we need to devote a bit of time to changing them or reprogramming them. They won't simply disappear just because we want them to.

Being aware of what our beliefs are is a great thing, but it's only the first step. Once we are aware of them, we then have to do something about the beliefs that need changing.

Many of us already have all the tools, the knowledge and the ability to change our beliefs. We don't need anyone else to help us; we just need to want to do it enough to take the necessary action.

What do **YOU** believe?

That you're unlucky in love?

That you're useless at managing or making money?

That you'll never be happy?

That you'll never be good enough?

That you'll always be a failure?

Whatever the belief is, it **CAN** be changed.

You are **NOT** stuck with it!

Find a way to release it and then choose your new beliefs with care. Choose ones that support you, and that help you create the life of your dreams. You might be reading this and thinking ...

*It's fine for you to say that, but **HOW**?*

Chances are that if you're reading this, you're a self-help-book junkie! You're likely to have all the reprogramming methods and belief-releasing tools you need already. Just dig into your library of books, pick a process and try it out.

As with the process of elimination to find your method, if it doesn't work, try a different one. And if you want a really simple method to try, check out Reprogram The Mind (page 26).

It's Just The Way I Am

Along with the beliefs you formed by the time you were seven, over the course of your life you will have formed stories around who you are – based on what has happened to you in the past and what you think may be going to happen to you in the future. These stories are told by yourself to yourself and others through your words and actions, and you will repeat them over and over and manifest them in your life in every way possible.

Because these stories **ARE** you. They are **WHO YOU ARE**, and that's just the way it is. And based on your past experiences, that's the way things will always be for you.

But that's not true. They are **NOT** you.

They are simply stories. They are your perception of what has happened to you, where you have been, what you have done. They are not the absolute truth. They are just … words, ideas, thoughts. Your stories do not define you, and they should not limit you.

YOU ARE PERFECT!

YOU ARE UNLIMITED!

Horror Stories

You can choose to tell another story. You can dial into another frequency. You can change the channel. If you hated horror movies would you insist on watching the horror channel every day? I hope not. Because why would you want to do that to yourself?

Yet you continue to tell horror stories about your health, your relationships and your career failures, all in the name of connecting with another human over how terrible it all is, or using your stories as an example of how much more pathetic or unlucky you are than everyone else.

STOP IT!

Write a new story.

Start telling it with conviction, and it will become your reality. Believe it. Live it. Breathe it. And if the people around you don't like the new story, find people who do.

It takes effort to catch yourself before you start retelling the old stories. It takes imagination to see the new story as being real before it has fully manifested. But it's so worth it when it begins to happen around you and you realize that you don't even miss the old stories because they never made you happy anyway.

Oh Shit! It's Raining Again

Yes, you've guessed the topic of this section.

COMPLAINING.

One of the biggest obstacles in changing our lives is our love of complaining. Many people love to complain, especially about things they cannot control, like the weather. There is so much in our lives that we **CAN** control, but rather than change things, we would prefer simply to complain about it.

Complaining elicits sympathy and empathy from others. It reinforces our victim mentality – that we haven't got the life/body/career/health we want because life is simply unfair to us – and it's not our fault.

Well, it's not anybody else's fault either.

There's a fabulous video on YouTube of one of my favourite authors in the world, Neale Donald Walsch. He wrote the *Conversations with God* series of books, and in this particular video he makes one very simple point …

God (or the universe, spirit, whatever you want to call it) only ever says 'Yes'. Literally, yes to **EVERYTHING** you say. So every time you complain, God is agreeing with you and giving you **MORE** of it. Whatever you ask for, or talk about a lot, God thinks you want more of it. Interesting, huh?

Your complaints are basically requests to the universe to give you more stuff to complain about. If you love having a good moan, but you really **DO** want to change your life, then please watch the video. And if you need some help to stop complaining, then check out the book called *A Complaint Free World* by Will Bowen. It explains how to stop complaining, and challenges you to go 21 days in a row without a single complaint.

The antidote to complaining?

GRATITUDE.

Thank someone. Appreciate someone or something. Compliment someone. Count your blessings. See the silver lining.

The more you affirm all the good things in your life, the more good stuff will come to you.

Reprogram The Mind

If I had to recommend just one technique for reprogramming your mind, it would be EFT (Emotional Freedom Technique). Why this one? Because it's the **SIMPLEST**, **EASIEST** and **FASTEST** technique that I have seen make the most difference. In my own life and in the lives of others. So, give it a go. If it really doesn't work for you, then I'm sure you will find something else, but the point is to make the **EFFORT** to release your old beliefs and create new ones. They won't go away by themselves.

Yes, it might feel horrible, uncomfortable and painful during the process, but the alternative is to be miserable for the rest of your life. It's worth experiencing a short period of discomfort in order to create a better life, don't you think?

Work out who you want to be, what you want to do, where you want to go, the life you want to live, then begin to program those new thoughts, ideas and concepts into your mind, using the ultra-simple tool of EFT.

The process of EFT requires you simply to tap with your index finger on different points of your hand, face and body, while speaking your fears and affirmations out loud. The diagram opposite shows the different points, and the order to tap them in. So tap a few times on each point while stating a fear or issue. For example, let's take the fear of public speaking (I have used EFT very effectively for this).

While tapping on point 1, the side of your hand, say:
'Even though I'm afraid of speaking in front of a large audience, I completely love and accept myself.'

While tapping on point 2, next to your eyebrow, say:
'Even though I'm afraid of stuttering while speaking to a group of people, I completely love and accept myself.'

Tap on each point, and say out loud every possible fear or negative thought you have around the issue. When you run out, start affirming the positives. Continue tapping on each point while saying things like:
'I love talking to others about things I'm passionate about.'
'I am a confident public speaker.'

Keep going until you run out of positive things. This method can be used for anything. Any fear, any phobia, even physical issues. For further information on EFT and how to use it, check out *The Happiness Code* or *The Tapping Solution* or search for EFT videos on YouTube.

1   Side of Hand
2   Eyebrow
3   Side of Eye
4   Under Eye
5   Under Nose
6   Chin
7   Collar Bone
8   Crown

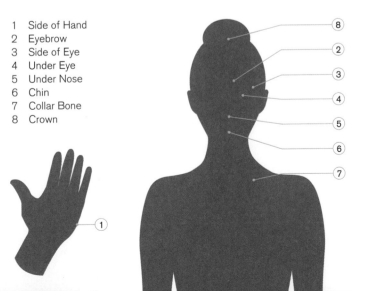

Better The Devil You Know

Ah, the comfort zone. So much is written about this cosy little place we love to live in. This comfortable place where everyone knows our name, where we have our spot, where we fit in — and usually it's the place where we're miserable, stuck in a toxic relationship and completely broke.

Why do we stay there? Because we know it so well. It's 'safe'. Making changes, releasing beliefs, trying new ideas, these are things that push us into the unknown and force us into a new way of being that we're just not used to.

As creatures of **HABIT**, this is **FUCKING SCARY**.

Sometimes, the comfort zone is actually quite a happy place, but it is not where growth happens; it's where everything pretty much stays the same.

But why do you think the saying is 'better the **DEVIL** you know'?

It's because the comfort zone sounds all lovely and cosy, but it's not. It's just what we are used to. In this comfortable space we will never truly know what we are capable of. And that makes me sad.

Get Off The Merry-Go-Round

One of the things that usually happens in our comfort zone is that we endlessly repeat certain patterns. We get stuck on a merry-go-round and won't get off until we're ill or have seriously had enough.

Breaking these cycles and patterns is tough. Trust me, I have been stuck in them. I have been aware of them and still done nothing about them. But, finally, I have managed to break them. I would say it takes sheer willpower, but that wouldn't be entirely accurate.

You also need a very good reason to break the cycle. If you don't, if there is enough good stuff to justify putting up with the bad stuff, then you will just keep going around and around on that painted horse.

For me, it was realizing that I didn't want to get to the end of **ANOTHER** year and find myself in the exact same place.

I wanted to evolve, grow, change.

I did **NOT** want to be stuck in the rut any longer.
So I took a deep breath, cut the ties, removed the
possibilities of falling back into the same space and moved
myself on.

Was it tough?

Yes.

Did I want to change my mind?

Yes.

Did I **SCREAM, SHOUT, CRY** and **HATE** it?

Yes.

But I did it anyway, because it was even more painful to
imagine staying in the same place.

It's a funny thing. Humans are far more likely to change
their lives by running away from pain than by running
towards joy. We're an odd bunch.

The pain was great enough that I finally said, 'I'm done!'
Time to change. I had no idea what I was moving towards; I
couldn't even picture a life that was free of the cycle. It was

just a big, blank canvas. It was a void. A terrifying, empty void. But I chose to dive into that void and to work on filling it with things that would bring me joy rather than staying where I was, repeating the same old cycles.

You can do it too. Anyone can. The best thing, would be to make the decision to leap **BEFORE** you have no other choice. But again, humans tend not to do that. We need to experience the darkest night of our soul, the lowest point of our existence, before we say ...

ENOUGH!

NO MORE!

Sad really. So, yeah, you might read this bit, shrug your shoulders and think, *Aww, the merry-go-round isn't so bad really. I'll stay a bit longer. You never know, it could change, it could get better and it could miraculously become something incredible, the best ride of my life!*

Spoiler alert:

IT WON'T.

But, hey, it's your journey. You'll move on when you're ready.

The Information Junkie

I'm an information junkie. Realizing this came as something of a revelation, and it occurred to me while reading yet another self-help book. I realized that I love to discover things that make me think:

HOLY SHIT!

That's why I am the way I am!

And I get all excited that I have found **THE THING** to change my life, and I have all these wonderful intentions to **ACTION** the exercises and **REALLY** make a difference this time. Then I put the book down, go, **WOW THAT WAS AMAZING**, and then resume my life as normal.

The funny thing is, I often pass on these amazing nuggets to people who then do something with them and change their lives. This used to make me feel like a failure. After all, I knew the same things they did, so why couldn't I change my life too? Because apparently I prefer just to read this stuff and store it away for a rainy day. Use it? **HAHAHAHAHA**. Yeah, right.

But do you know what? I also realized that part of my life's purpose is to share information with others, and that there's probably a **LOT** that I've learned and read that will never be useful to me, but I read it so I can pass it on and help someone else.

So, if you're an information junkie, be proud! You are likely to be helping others change their lives. But if it bugs you and you want to help yourself as well as others, you'd best read on.

You, Unplugged

If you feel you are drowning in information and are becoming overwhelmed, there's only one solution. It's a tough one, especially for junkies, but it's the only way.

DETOX.

Stop consuming information. Stop reading. Stop watching TED talks. Stop reading the articles that pop up on Facebook or Twitter or Tumblr. If you can't stop yourself from clicking, then go one step further and stay off the internet. Easier said than done, I know. I'm addicted to social media, and I'm not ashamed to admit it!

But if you are drowning in information, it really is the only way forward. Stop taking in any more information.

Start with a day of unplugging.

Then extend it to a week.

Spend some time with yourself, doing something creative, something fun or calming and peaceful, or something outright crazy. Spend time with friends – in person.
Mad idea, I know.

Just **STAY AWAY** from new information.

Even after detoxing you might realize you'll always be an information junkie – which is by no means the worst thing in the world to be – but just be sure you take regular breaks so that your brain doesn't explode.

Because that would be pretty gross and quite inconvenient for you.

Where's My Fxxking Unicorn?

The Actionless Hero

Inside us all is a little part that would quite like to be an action hero. To swoop in, save the day, rescue the girl/boy, stop the world from being destroyed — you know the score. Despite the widely held belief that only special people can do these things, I believe that we are all capable of being an action hero. We all have superpowers, and most of us know what they are, too.

But unless we use them, we will remain ordinary citizens.

There's a reason why an action hero is named thus. They take **ACTION**. They don't go, 'Oh look! That needs doing! Oh dear! That person needs saving!' No, they just do it. They take **ACTION**.

But there are many of us who are desperate to change, in chronic pain, longing for that life we dream of, and yet we take no action to sort it out. We just keep doing whatever we're currently doing — which clearly isn't working or we would be exactly where we wanted to be already!

So don't be an **ORDINARY CITIZEN**.

Be an **ACTION HERO**.

If it helps, get some superhero underpants. They'll make you feel awesome and spur you on. Honestly.

Just Fucking Do It

There's really no other solution to inaction than to JFDI.

Pick something you want to change, decide on a course of action and get started. Or pick a creative project you want to do and charge into it. You don't need all the info and know-how or the full plan. Just start, and then figure it out as you go along.

What are you waiting for?

JFDI!

And if you need some amusing encouragement, look up Art Williams's 'Just Do It' speech on YouTube. The video makes me chuckle and, despite the repetition of what he says, he makes an oh-so-brilliant point.

The Inconvenient Time

There is no right time. There is no good time.

There is only **NOW**. This moment. So **STOP WAITING**.

Stop waiting for the right time of year, the right season, when you feel fully prepared or when the inspiration hits.

Stop waiting for him to get a clue, stop waiting for her to notice you.

Just **STOP WAITING.**

And take action. What do you do if an amazing idea for a book comes to you when your to-do list is ten pages long, work is coming out of your ears and you need to go food shopping? Start writing the book! Now! Because there will never be a perfect time to write it.

BUT THERE IS RIGHT NOW.

You want to leave the toxic relationship, but it's their birthday next week? Leave! Because after that it will be Christmas, then Valentine's Day, then, oh, look, it's their birthday again! Can't leave now!

You want to strike out on your own and start your own business, but you don't feel qualified enough or there's a recession or the exchange rate is bad?

Start it now! There really is no better time.

These are all excuses. They don't matter. If there is something you need to do, if you are passionate about something or if the words are flowing effortlessly through your brain, then get to it!

Oh, and the solution to waiting? JFDI.

To-Do List, Or Not To-Do List?

If you've read as many self-help books as I have, you will undoubtedly have read the conflicting advice regarding to-do lists. Some books suggest doing a brain dump of everything you want to accomplish, then picking out a few things to get done in the next day or week or month. Some advocate choosing just three things a day. Some say you should create a list the night before so you can get going first thing in the morning. Others say that to-do lists are evil and should be avoided at all costs.

So what is the right answer? Should we have a to-do list or not? My answer? There is no right answer. If having a to-do list works for you, then have one; if it doesn't, then don't. Simple really. In fact, you could apply that advice to pretty much anything in your life.

Personally, I need lists. Not as motivational tools as such, but to back up my pretty terrible memory. I can have an idea and, just minutes later, have absolutely no idea what it was. If I don't write it down in that magical moment it will be lost forever. I will remember **HAVING** the idea but not what the idea was.

Without my to-do lists, I'm a bit lost. I have lists on my whiteboard, on my phone, in my organizer, in random sketchbooks, on the back of my hand …

That Is The Question

I really quite enjoy the feeling of ticking completed items off my to-do lists. It gives me that warm feeling of satisfaction that I have actually achieved something with my day or my week. But then there is the reverse side, where you discover a brain dump from three years ago and realize that nearly everything on it is **STILL** on your current list, and you begin to wonder what the hell is wrong with you.

Of course, nothing is wrong with you. Things happen at the perfect time and not a moment before. (This is where believing in the spiritual concept of divine timing comes in handy.) So, as discussed in Method In Your Madness (page 14), go with what works. If having a to-do list rocks your world, then please keep doing it; if it drains the life out of your beautiful soul, then ditch it and find a new approach.

When it comes to being productive and getting things done, my best advice would be to keep it simple. The more complicated your to-do list is, the more likely you will spend more time on creating or upkeeping the list than you will doing the tasks on it. So, find the simplest possible way of managing a list that works for you.

Oh, and one last thing. Get some stickers and coloured pens. After all, just because a to-do list needs to be functional, it doesn't mean it can't be stylish and fun, too!

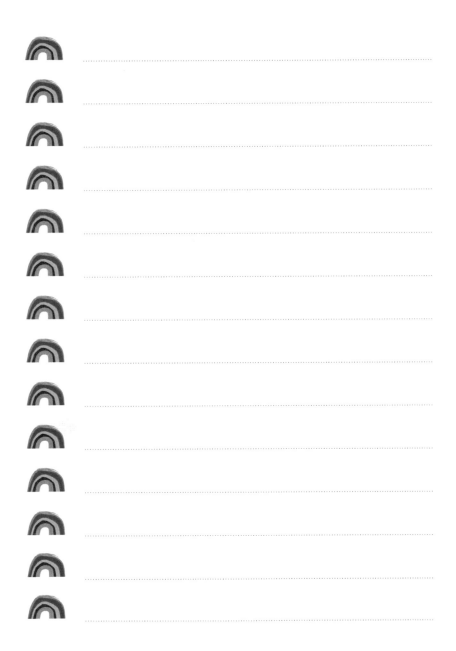

Essential Juggling 101

Many people want to write books. I should know, I was one of them. But only a fraction of those novelist wannabes actually sit down and get the words out. Why? Because most people have their priorities messed up.

It's not their fault, it's just that modern living requires you to juggle a gazillion balls while simultaneously spinning ten billion plates, so something like writing a book, learning to play the guitar or travelling around the world just gets put last on the list.

But, as we know, the last thing on the list never gets done. Only the essential things get done. We will always find the time, energy and strength to do what is essential, because our survival depends on it. We're less likely to find the time and energy to do things that may nourish our souls but aren't essential for our physical survival.

Writing a book is not essential. In fact, it could even be detrimental in the short term, especially if you are writing instead of food shopping or sleeping or working to pay your bills. But, if you don't prioritize your passion/mission/purpose, you will never do it.

Making it a priority means not letting days, weeks, months go by without doing something about it. It means not letting decades go by without having achieved the things you most want to do with your life.

It's Not In My Stars

I'm really into spiritual stuff. I've read a million books (slight exaggeration, but not by much), I've attended seminars, I read oracle cards, I even write novels on spiritual subjects. I'm really, **REALLY** into it. But sometimes, spiritual stuff offers more excuses than solutions. These, for example:

- My star sign is not very outgoing, so I couldn't possibly become a public speaker.

- I had my astrological chart read, and it seems I'm not meant to start a business this year.

- My psychic told me that I would meet my soulmate in the next five years, so if it's going to happen anyway I don't have to work on myself/my appearance/my old baggage, etc.

- My tarot reading said it was a really bad idea to break up right now.

- Mercury is in retrograde.

- It's a full moon.

Okay, so some of these examples are a bit silly, but do you see where I'm heading here? Spiritual stuff is great for helping you to bring calm and peace into your life, to explore fun concepts and ideas such as parallel universes or telepathy or healing, and there are so many awesome tools to heal your body and create the life you want.

But it's all too easy to use spirituality as an excuse **NOT** to act, as a reason **NOT** to push forward, and it can end up becoming a hindrance.

Don't do that.

Knowing The Future

For a few years I was really into getting readings with mediums, psychics and tarot readers. I was desperate to know my future, to find out what my path was, to see what was coming up. But when several readings all said the same thing, I thought: *Oh, shit. I don't want that.*

And so I went into resistance mode, trying my best to do everything possible to make sure the scenario wouldn't happen. As a result of my resistance, I was unable to be happy. Because I wasn't choosing what I wanted or what would be good for me. I was simply choosing things that would ensure that the predicted path would never be mine. How ridiculous.

I realized that I needed to stop having readings. Now, whenever a psychic friend offers any guidance, I quite happily say: 'I don't want to know. I want to remain in the now, make decisions in the best way I can in the moment. I want to use my own knowledge, tune into my own intuition and listen to myself. I trust myself.' And so far, so good.

Psychics can only see the most likely path in that particular moment. You are the author of your own life. You are the creator of your own destiny. No one else is. So start listening to yourself and make your own path.

Go on a spiritual detox, and **STOP** using predictions as an **EXCUSE** not to do what you really want to do.

Clowns To The Left ...

Most of the time we resist changing our lives because we are worried about changing as a person and becoming a different version of ourselves. And that version might not get on very well with our spouses, families, siblings, friends, colleagues and the rest. So, rather than risking the change and moving forward, we remain the same. This is a tricky one. I can't tell you to ditch everyone who loves you, find a whole new group of friends or create a new family because that's so drastic that you'll never do it. But you can start to hang out with a different crowd. You can spend time with people who are where you want to be, not where you are trying to move away from.

Jim Rohn said that you become the average of the five people you spend most of your time with, and your income will become an average of the incomes of those five people, too. Considering how successful he was as an author and motivational speaker, I would say he was worth listening to.

So, if you're broke, seek out more affluent people. If your friends are very negative, seek out more positive friendships. If you're starting a business, find other people who have successfully set up businesses.

It's good to be around people on the same path so you can help each other and keep each other accountable, but make sure there are people further ahead, too, so you can move towards where they are.

... Jokers To The Right

Yes, you may lose friends. Yes, your relationship may not survive. Yes, your sibling may stop speaking to you. But the alternative is to do nothing, to stay where you are.

And I **KNOW** that if you have read as many self-help books as I think you have, and judging by the fact you are reading this book right now ...

You **WANT** to fucking **CHANGE**!

Change can be painful and upsetting. But it is not forever. You will find that you create new, stronger relationships. Once you have created what you want and have got to the place that feels good to you, you may even find that you inspire your old friends who might then rejoin your life.

Anything is possible, but you have to be prepared to be alone, to lose people and to make new friends and contacts if you want to find your fucking unicorn.

Lean On Me

Finding a mentor is one of the things that most self-help/business books suggest. Get a coach, get a mentor. Find someone who believes in you. It's sound advice. But it might not always be practical advice.

For a start, it can be expensive. Then, there's choosing the right one. How do you know that their method will work for you? How do you know you will see any improvement in your health/business/career/relationship? How do you know it will be worth the money? You don't.

But, as we saw in Method In Your Madness (page 14), you just have to give it a go. Listen to your gut, go with someone who is walking their talk, who is genuine and who really wants to see you succeed, not someone who wants to sign you up just to get a load of cash out of you.

And if you really can't afford it, find a Facebook group that offers free mentoring or coaching or guidance, or find someone who is willing to exchange their time in return for something you can offer.

Most coaches and mentors are passionate about helping others to shine and reach their true potential, so they often create affordable options for you to be able to access their genius and wisdom.

I would highly recommend George Hardwick, author of *Creative Uprising* and creator of the Creative Ignition course. George is incredibly talented in many creative pursuits, but one of his specialities is seeing **YOUR** unique talent, and helping you to get it out into the world. With his support and encouragement, you will feel like you can conquer the world. And **THAT'S** the kind of influence you need.

Having someone who believes in you is invaluable, because in those dark moments when it seems just too damned hard to be on this planet, they will be the one to say, 'I believe you can do this.'

I know that what you have to do and share is important, so get off your butt and **JFDI**. And just in case you don't find the right coach or mentor, I want to say to you, from my heart to yours …

YOU CAN DO THIS.

I BELIEVE IN YOU.

Now, get started.

It's Got To Be Perfect

Perfectionism should be classed as a dirty, rude, bad word. Because it really is a bastard. How much do people leave undone simply because they feel too inadequate to do it perfectly? I shudder to think.

I will tell you right now that **NOTHING** is perfect.

And yet, paradoxically, **EVERYTHING** is perfect, because everything is perfect in its imperfection.

That may be too woo woo for you, but it's true, I promise.

You should stop trying to get perfectly straight lines, waiting until you have ten more qualifications or until you have enough experience or whatever. It will never be perfect. You will never be perfect and, as we've discussed, it will never be the perfect time and the planets will never be perfectly aligned.

Do it **IMPERFECTLY**.

Joyfully.

Wildly.

With gleeful abandon.

Of course, I'm talking about creative pursuits here, not brain surgery. If you're a brain surgeon, for goodness' sake, please do strive for something close to perfection. (And please wait until you're qualified.) But even then, you won't be perfect.

That's what it means to be human. If we wanted perfection we would never have come to this planet. We came here to experience the mess, the wonkiness, the scribbles and the chaos. Enjoy it, make a beautiful mess and stop worrying about making it perfect. It's a waste of your precious time.

A book that has inspired me in this area is *The Gifts of Imperfection* by Brené Brown. Brené is the queen of vulnerability, being a shame researcher and now an author and public speaker.

She knows how to dare greatly and have fun in the process.

Monsters In The Closet

We couldn't have a self-help book without the worst F-word ever: **FEAR**

There are so many books out there on conquering fear and how to be brave and courageous in the face of the demons and the monsters in our closet. But even after reading them all, we're still riddled with fear.

I know I don't need to explain what fear is. You already know it intimately. I know you do, otherwise you wouldn't be stuck where you are. You wouldn't be reading this book. You would be living, acting on your dreams, working towards a life filled with passion and purpose and joy. So, yeah. Fear. We all have it. It's a part of being human. And do you know what? It's a **GOOD THING**.

I can imagine the look on your face right now. It's quite funny. Fear is good. It's brilliant, in fact. Because when your tummy flips, and you feel like you might start to hyperventilate, and you want to throw up ... you have just hit on something that you need to face. That you need to heal. That you really need to do.

Your fear is just a way of your inner child/higher self/
guardian angel telling you: 'This is important. Take note'.

If you felt no fear, if things were easy, if you were blasé
about it all, how would you know what the good stuff was?
The important stuff? We've all experienced that moment
of triumph when we feel terrified but go for it anyway and
then come out the other side feeling invincible. If we felt
no fear we would feel no triumph.

And that sounds pretty sucky to me.

So love your fear. Love the monsters in the closet. Most
of them are probably cute and fluffy anyway.

Love The Shadows

Every human is made up of light and shadows, and we need both sides to be balanced. When you get into spiritual stuff, it seems like it's all about staying positive no matter what, about releasing/eliminating/getting rid of the bad stuff.

But to be whole, we need all of it. So, it's not about hating your dark side, it's about accepting it and making friends with it. Like the fear, it is telling you something.

When you get angry, understand that whatever angered you could be a trigger. Maybe it means that your purpose in this life is to do something about it, or maybe it means that you were just angry in that moment. Not everything has to have a deep, spiritual meaning; some things are just the way they are. But for goodness' sake, love it all, because love really is the answer.

Feel afraid? Love feeling afraid.

Feel angry? Love the anger.

Feel sad? Love the expression of grief in the form of tears.

Allow yourself to feel, to experience, to express every side of yourself, every emotion. You're here on this planet for all those things, not just to prance about singing happy songs and thinking happy thoughts.

As you start to love all of yourself, the light and the shadows, you may even find that you spend more time in the light than the shadows, but even if you don't, it doesn't matter.

What matters is that it's all good. All of it. Even when it seems like it's all shit.

Honestly.

What can you love about yourself right now, that you have been fighting, hating or resenting? Treat it like a fluffy rainbow unicorn kitten and give it some love right now.

Drama Llama

It was only very recently I discovered that I am a drama llama. I looooove the drama. Why else would I remain in situations filled with drama, surround myself with drama-filled people and seek to be the helper of all drama llamas? Only one reason. I am a drama llama.

And that's why my life is not calm and peaceful, with me sat at a lovely desk, overlooking the beach, writing my books in quiet solitude while my partner brings me snacks.

Because there's **NO DRAMA** in that!

Now, being a writer, I realize that my desire for drama is (in a way) one of my methods for finding inspiration for my stories. After all, no one reads books where the protagonist lives a life of blissful harmony. Where's the fun in that? Humans thrive on drama. Why else would they watch the news or be taken in by the clickbait articles on Facebook?

Drama is great because it is entertaining. It provides mad stories that we can share. It can give us something more interesting to talk about than the weather. It is not great, however, when it's basically just a distraction. When it becomes a form of procrastination that takes you away from your purpose. So, if you are a drama llama – that's okay, embrace and love the part of you that loves the drama. Just don't let it stop you from living the life you really want.

When You Can't See The Floor For The Pants

The biggest distraction and time-suck in my life is undoubtedly clutter. The stuff that surrounds me that needs sorting, tidying, sifting through – my clutter has wasted much of my time. I am, of course, grateful for all the things I have, but I have had a tendency to keep stuff long after it should have been donated or burned, and then I wonder why I cannot find anything.

The items in your room, your house and your life should be beautiful, loved, functional, useful and have their own place. If things don't fit into these categories, they are simply a hindrance to you.

I know that I have trouble getting rid of stuff at times, but when I read *The Life-Changing Magic of Tidying*, I knew I wanted to change.

I took action after reading that book. I donated three bags of clothes and several boxes of books to charity and burned three black bags of old paperwork, and was then able to fit all of my day-to-day possessions into my small car. Which makes moving much easier (and I do move a lot).

How did it inspire me to take action? Quite honestly, the author, Marie Kondo, explained the process in a way that made total sense to me. When I described it to a friend who is incredibly neat and tidy, she replied with, 'That's how my brain works!'

Well, it's not how my brain works! But when I read an explanation of how it's possible to declutter that made sense to me, I found that I was able to take action and make it happen.

I still have a lot of stuff stored away that needs sorting, but I made a great start on it and felt so much better for it, too. I find that a bit of chaotic mess can help creativity, but mountains of it halts it altogether.

The **BALANCE** needs to be right.

Get rid of some junk, and, if you need a push, read Marie's book. It sold millions of copies for a reason.

Why So Serious?

I kept the best to last. I have one final thing to say:

Life is meant to be **FUN**!

Honestly, we all get so serious about stuff, and we think that being a grown-up is about leaving behind play, exploration and joyfulness. But it's not. Humans of all ages need to have fun. And, in fact, the more fun things are, the more likely we are to succeed. Want to write a book? Get a silly hat to wear while writing and a new pen or a notebook with unicorns on it to write it in. Why? Because it makes it more fun.

A friend of mine in the USA works from home, and we often lament to each other on Facebook about how bored we are (as we have little daily human interaction in person), and how dull it is wading through our to-do lists, and how much we are lacking in motivation. So, we created a game.

We assigned points to each task on our lists, and then each day we get points for the things we get done. The points relate to the difficulty of the tasks and the length of time they take. Then we aim for a daily and monthly goal.

It sounds silly, but it really works. We find ourselves pushing through the boredom and the lack of motivation just because we want to win!

Turn things into a game. Turn cleaning the house into a game. Turn starting your own business into a game.

I knew that I wanted to become more organized, but I had never managed to keep a diary past the end of January before. So I bought a pretty organizer, named her Astrid, and bought some funky purple pens, unicorn stickers and pretty paper inserts. This encouraged me actually to use the diary, and I ended up doing so for the whole year. And every year since. Being on top of things does not have to be dull. In fact, it should be anything but.

One of my favourite self-help books is *Ask and It Is Given* by Esther and Jerry Hicks. Half of the book is filled with fun exercises and games to get you into a flowing, relaxed and happy state of manifesting. Check it out if you're stumped on how to make taking action more fun.

So ... play, have fun, give yourself star stickers when you complete a task. There's a reason why children have more enthusiasm and excitement when doing things; it's because they make it into a game, and they love to get rewards and treats for doing things well.

We all have inner children who are desperate to play.

LET THEM!

IS THAT
MY FUCKING
UNICORN?

It's time to accept your reality. To acknowledge where you are, and that **YOU** got yourself there. You cannot change what you cannot accept. So, accept it.

This means taking responsibility for your actions, thoughts and stories so far. It means you are not fighting what is, because that will never get you anywhere.

With this awareness you can begin to make changes and move towards where you would rather be.

It means that you actually will change. And in order to get to where you want to go, you have to know where you are now.

Acceptance also brings forgiveness – for yourself, for your actions and for the actions of others. Because you are only where you are as a result of all that has gone before, and where you are is perfect. There's no need to blame anyone for anything. Including yourself.

The other awesome thing about living in acceptance of what is, is that it reduces stress. You can only be stressed when you are fighting reality. When you don't want it to be raining, when you don't want to be late, when you're annoyed that someone didn't do what they said they would. When you accept these things exactly as they are, then there's no stress. Which means you are calm and relaxed and able to see how to sort things out.

No stress. Just solutions.

Ideas don't come at convenient times, they come at the **RIGHT** time. They come when you are open to them, when you are relaxed, joyful, happy.

Ideas don't appear when you stare at a blank screen, yelling for inspiration. Money doesn't appear when you are staring at your empty wallet or the minus sign on your bank statement while crying out in desperation. The perfect relationship doesn't appear when you are sat at a bar, staring morosely into your beer, dwelling on your shitty love life.

Everything comes to us when we are relaxed and flowing. Inspiration comes to us in the shower, while washing up, while walking along, while doing nothing in particular, while being happy in ourselves, while doing things we love.

Do whatever you need to do to get to that place of relaxed flow. The power to change your life is entirely in your hands.

You might get to the end of this book, put it down, and say:

THIS IS GOING TO CHANGE MY LIFE! EVERYTHING WILL BE DIFFERENT NOW!

And then find that after a few days the joy and motivation has waned and dissipated and you are repeating the same patterns, telling the same stories and perpetuating the same life you had before.

THAT IS OK.

You are human. It happens. This book will probably not change the lives of millions. But if one person acts on any of the solutions offered and changes just 2% of their life because of these words, then I consider my job done.

I haven't written this book to change your life. Only **YOU** can change your life. I wrote it to explore ideas, possibilities and random wonderings. Whether you do something or nothing with the information is entirely up to you.

But remember, unicorns are rare creatures that live in magical places, and if you don't get off your butt and take action, then you will never find your fucking unicorn.

You will remain an ordinary citizen forever.

If that doesn't spur you on to make some changes, nothing will.

Further Reading

Chris Baty, *No Plot? No Problem!: A Low-Stress, High-Velocity Guide To Writing A Novel In 30 Days* (Chronicle Books, 2004)

Will Bowen, *A Complaint Free World: The 21-Day Challenge That Will Change Your Life* (Virgin Books, 2007)

Brené Brown, *The Gifts of Imperfection: Let Go Of Who You Think You're Supposed To Be And Embrace Who You Are* (Hazelden FIRM, 2010)

Rhonda Byrne, *The Secret* (Atria Books, 2006)

Rhonda Byrne, *The Power* (Atria Books, 2010)

Rhonda Byrne, *The Magic* (Atria Books, 2012)

Kyle Cease, *I Hope I Screw This Up: How Falling In Love With Your Fears Can Change The World* (North Star Way, 2017)

Oriah Mountain Dreamer, *The Call: Discovering Why You Are Here* (Element, 2010)

Debbie Ford, *Dark Side of The Light Chasers: Reclaiming Your Power, Creativity, Brilliance, And Dreams* (Hodder, 2001)

George Hardwick, *Creative Uprising: How To Make A Living And Make A Difference Doing What You Love* (Panoma Press Ltd, 2013)

Esther Hicks and Jerry Hicks, *Ask And It Is Given: Learning To Manifest The Law Of Attraction* (Hay House, 2010)

Marie Kondo, *The Life-Changing Magic of Tidying: A Simple, Effective Way To Banish Clutter Forever* (Vermillion, 2014)

Dr Gary Laundre and Lloyd Richmond, *The Happiness Code* (Richmond House, 2010)

Nick Ortner, *The Tapping Solution: A Revolutionary System For Stress-Free Living* (Hay House, 2013)

Websites

Neale Donald Walsch, *God Says Yes*
www.youtube.com/watch?v=ZMPhTLez_Ck

Art Williams, *Just Do It*
www.youtube.com/watch?v=TU7Y6HiLXto

National Novel Writing Month
www.nanowrimo.org & www.campnanowrimo.org

George Hardwick, The Creative Uprising
www.creativeuprising.com

About The Author

Michelle Gordon is a writer, photographer, self-confessed drama llama and self-help junkie. From a young age, her ultimate unicorn was to be an author, and she began writing novels in 2009. Michelle writes about angels, faeries, aliens, parallel universes, spirits and alternate dimensions.

Michelle has so far penned two fiction collections, totalling twelve books. Her Visionary Collection contains a novella called *Heaven dot com* as well as three novels: *The Doorway to PAM*, *The Elphite* and *I'm Here*. These stand-alone stories deal with down-to-earth characters who find themselves in out-of-this-world circumstances. Warning: do not read without a box of tissues nearby. You'll need them.

The Earth Angel series consists of eight novels: *The Earth Angel Training Academy, The Earth Angel Awakening, The Other Side, The Twin Flame Reunion, The Twin Flame Retreat, The Twin Flame Resurrection, The Twin Flame Reality* and *The Twin Flame Rebellion*. As long as the faeries and angels keep bringing the snacks and stories, the series will continue!

Michelle is a bit of a Jane-of-all-trades, and loves to try new things. She loves creating, and her favourite crafts are crocheting, sewing, scrapbooking, painting and making jewellery. She is a keen photographer, and loves to photograph nature, animals and occasionally people. To see her favourite photos, follow her on Instagram! (@michellegordonauthor). Michelle also loves to bake and has a lot of fun experimenting since she is a gluten-free, dairy-free veggie, who loves cake!

You can also find out more about Michelle on her website – MichelleGordon.co.uk and on her blog – TwinFlameBlog.com. If you would like to become an Earth Angel Trainee, you can join the online Earth Angel Training Academy. Visit: EarthAngelAcademy.co.uk to enrol.

Acknowledgements

When you have as many unicorns to chase as I do, it's important to have awesome friends and family who support the crazy dreams, and I have to say, I have the most awesome team of people around me.

So I would like to express my love and gratitude to these incredible people, because they rock.

Mum, you are the one who has believed in me, loved me, supported and encouraged me my whole life, and I know that I have only achieved what I have because I was loved unconditionally. Thank you, I love you so much.

Jon, you've always encouraged me to chase even the craziest of unicorns, and have always believed that I am capable of achieving anything I set my mind to. Thank you for your love and support. I love you.

Liz Lockwood, my best friend, editor and cheerleader. Without you, the shadows might well have taken over and I am so grateful to have you in my life. You are amazing, I love you.

Liz Gordon, you have never told me I am crazy, even when I feel it must be true. Instead, you have said — we can make this work. I love you for encouraging me and supporting me to find my unicorn.

The following people have been a part of the unicorn journey, and they each know how they have impacted my life, but I haven't got enough space to write it all here! (If you find your name on this list and you don't know how amazing and important you are to me, then call me and I will be happy to tell you!)

Mr Bee, Annette Ecuyere, Helen Gordon, Sarah Rebecca Vine, Kelly Draper, Tiffany Hathorn, Niki, Xander, Nicole Brookdale, Lucja Fratczak-Kay, Philip James, Andrew Embling, Marc Gordon, John Byrne, Laurie Huston, Margaux Joy DeNador, James John Malaniak, Trisha & Bruce Barnes, Kariel Tejai and Keith Higgs.